LANGUAGE ARTS EXPLORER

USING ALTERNATIVE ENERGIES

by Courtney Farrell

CHERRY LAKE PUBLISHING • ANN ARBOR, MICHIGAN

Published in the United States of America
by Cherry Lake Publishing
Ann Arbor, Michigan
www.cherrylakepublishing.com

Printed in the United States of America

January 2010
CLSP06

Consultants: Jeff Clark, associate professor of geology, Lawrence University; Gail Saunders-Smith, associate professor of literacy, Beeghly College of Education, Youngstown State University

Editorial direction:
Melissa Johnson

Book design and illustration:
Becky Daum

Photo credits: Katrin Solansky/iStockphoto, cover, 1; Frank van Haalen/iStockphoto, 5; James Richey/iStockphoto, 7; Dorling Kindersley, 9; Fotolia, 11; Eliza Snow/iStockphoto, 12; Hazlan Abdul Hakim/iStockphoto, 15; iStockphoto, 17, 21, 24; Gene Chutka/iStockphoto, 19; Scott Cressman/iStockphoto, 23; Otmar Smit/iStockphoto, 27

Library of Congress Cataloging-in-Publication Data
Farrell, Courtney.
  Save the planet : using alternative energies / by Courtney Farrell.
    p. cm. — (Language arts explorer)
  Includes bibliographical references and index.
  ISBN 978-1-60279-663-8 (hardback) — ISBN 978-1-60279-672-0 (pbk.)
 1. Renewable energy sources—Juvenile literature. I. Title. II. Series.

 TJ808.2.F47 2010
 333.79'4—dc22

                                          2009038099

Cherry Lake Publishing would like to acknowledge the work of The Partnership for 21st Century Skills. Please visit www.21centuryskills.org for more information.

TABLE OF CONTENTS

You are being given a mission. The facts in **What You Know** will help you accomplish it. Remember **What You Know** while you are reading the story. The story will help you answer the questions at the end of the book. Have fun on this adventure!

Your mission is to investigate energy. All the machines we use need energy. Lights shine, computers hum, and people drive cars everywhere. Does this mean there is plenty of energy? On this mission, we will learn about some problems with the energy we use. Be sure to remember facts from What You Know as you read.

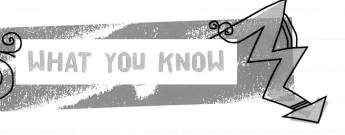

WHAT YOU KNOW

★ Fossil fuels include coal, oil, and natural gas. Fossil fuels are made from the remains of ancient plant and animal life. That is how they got the name *fossil*. Some fuels, such as natural gas, take millions of years to form. We use up fossil fuels much more quickly than they are replaced. They are nonrenewable resources.

★ Some fossil fuels create smoke when they are burned. This smoke can pollute the air. Breathing polluted air is bad for our health and for other living creatures.

Burning fossil fuels creates pollution.

★ The climate of Earth is changing. Most scientists agree that burning fossil fuels is making the changes worse.

★ Alternative energies such as solar and wind power are renewable. Renewable energies will never run out. They also produce less pollution.

We are going to take a field trip. We'll find out about all the different kinds of alternative energy. Come join us. Our first trip is to the Arctic. We're going across the North Pole in a helicopter!

We're here in the Arctic to learn about climate change. Around the world, the weather and climate are changing. Some warm places are becoming hotter. Some cool, forested places might turn to deserts. Farmers could have problems growing food. Scientists believe that people's actions have caused climate change or made natural climate change worse.

People and the Climate

How might people cause climate change? When people burn fossil fuels, a gas called carbon dioxide goes into the air with the smoke. Carbon dioxide is called a greenhouse gas. Greenhouse gases trap heat in our atmosphere. It's like putting a blanket around Earth. The whole planet warms up. This is called the greenhouse effect. It works like a greenhouse that warms up when the sun shines in. You have probably felt the greenhouse effect by getting into a car that got too hot from sitting in the sun. Some of the greenhouse effect is natural. It allows life to exist on the planet. However, too much trapped heat could become a problem.

Melting sea ice threatens polar bears.

Climate in the Arctic

Our field team came to the frozen North to learn about climate change. The effects of climate change are easy to see in cold places like the Arctic. Animals here are used to the cold. Many of them need floating rafts of sea ice to survive. Even in summer, the Arctic Ocean should have ice floating on it. The ice is melting now. Every year there is less ice than the year before.

Melting ice is a problem because seals and walruses come out of the water to rest on sea ice. Polar bears rest and hunt on sea ice, too. If the ice melts, polar bears can't hunt seals. Bears look for food in towns instead. Hungry bears can be a big problem for people in Arctic villages. We saw two polar bears eating garbage at the town dump today. People leave the bears alone when they see them. Polar bears can be dangerous!

Problems for People

Many scientists are afraid that climate change will cause problems for humans, too. One big issue is melting glaciers. Glaciers are huge, slow-moving ice masses.

PIKAS NEED COOL TEMPERATURES TO SuRVIVE

Pikas are small mammals with rounded ears that live high in the Rocky Mountains. Pikas are threatened by climate change. They need cool temperatures to survive. When the climate gets warmer, pikas move higher on their mountain slopes. Once they get to the top of the mountain there is nowhere else to go. If it gets too hot, they might even die.

Greenhouse gases trap heat from sunlight.

Scientists worry that water from melting glaciers around the world could make sea levels rise. This means oceans will be deeper, and cities near oceans might flood during storms. Some low-lying islands might go underwater completely!

We can help solve this problem by using less energy. We can also choose alternative energies instead of fossil fuels. At our next stop, we'll learn about some ways to save energy. ★

Our field team has traveled a long way. Now we're much farther south. We're visiting New Mexico in the southwestern part of the United States. We're here to see a very special house. The house is made specially to save energy.

Why Save Energy?

A lot of energy is used to heat homes in the winter and cool them in the summer. We already know that burning fossil fuels may increase climate change. There are other reasons to save energy. Fossil fuels such as oil and natural gas are called nonrenewable resources, because they won't last forever. Oil and other fossil fuels are found in the ground. People have already found and used up a lot of the oil that was easy to get. Now, people are finding more oil in hard-to-reach places, like under the ocean floor. It costs more money to find this oil and pump it out of the ground. It will be a long time before the last of the oil is gone, but oil prices will probably keep going up.

Power plants make electricity far away from our homes. Many power plants burn fossil fuels. The plants send electricity to us through power lines. We don't see

Some features of passive solar houses include solar panels and big windows to let in sunlight.

smoke billow out when we turn on our lights. The pollution comes out of the smokestack back at the power plant. We all share one atmosphere, so this pollutes the air for us all.

Passive Solar Houses

The house we are visiting is a passive solar house. Passive solar houses save energy and they save the owners lots of money, too. Today it was a hot summer day in New Mexico. Winter will be cold, though. This house will stay comfortable inside all year round, without mechanical heating or cooling.

How does passive solar design work? First, the house has thick walls and very good insulation. The walls are sealed tightly so air doesn't escape accidentally. This helps the house stay the same temperature. The house has air vents so people can control when air enters or leaves the building.

Let the Light In

The windows are placed so that the sun shines in a lot during the winter but shines in less during the summer. This keeps the house warmer when it's cold outside and

Oil and other fossil fuels are nonrenewable resources.

KEEPING THE HEAT

At the end of a sunny day, try touching a sidewalk or a big rock. It will still feel warm for a long time after the sun goes down. This is because it has thermal mass. Passive solar houses use heavy stone floors or thick walls to provide thermal mass. A material that has thermal mass will soak up heat from the sun during the day and store it for later. At night it cools off slowly, giving up its heat to warm the house.

colder when it's warm outside. Trees also help keep the house comfortable all year. Leafy trees are planted on the south side of the house. Their leaves shade the house in summer. These trees lose their leaves in winter, so the warm sun can shine in the windows.

Passive solar homes also use "daylighting" to save electricity. This means that light comes in through windows and skylights, so electric lights are shut off during the day. The result is less energy use and a lower electricity bill.

Even if you don't have a passive solar house, you can use these ideas, too. In the winter, you can open curtains and let the sun shine in. At night, you can close the curtains to save heat. In the summer, closing the curtains will keep the hot sun out. You'll help your parents save money, and help the planet, too! *

People use energy to do many things, not just heat and cool homes. Our next step is to learn how to save energy in our daily lives. The amount of energy a person uses is called a carbon footprint. A carbon footprint is a measure of the tons of carbon dioxide each person puts off in a year through his or her energy use. A carbon footprint includes energy used in the home and energy used for transportation. It even includes energy used to make and ship the food and everything else that a person uses.

A Family Saves Energy

Our field team is visiting a family in Utah. This family wanted to make their carbon footprint smaller. They wanted to save energy in the house they already owned. It's not a passive solar house, but they still save energy in a lot of other ways. They taught us how to do it, too!

We discovered that we could save a lot of energy by replacing regular round lightbulbs with spiral-shaped compact fluorescents. These bulbs stay cool and use less electricity. What a bright idea!

Bicycling instead of taking a car is one way to save energy.

By Foot or by Bike

Another way we learned to reduce our carbon footprint is by walking or riding a bike whenever we can. Cars use gasoline, which is a fossil fuel. The pollution from cars also contains greenhouse gases. Now we take the bus on longer trips. We drive a car only when we have to. We also pay attention to where our food and the other things we buy come from. We try to buy local goods that take shorter trips to get to us. ★

MORE GREEN-LIVING TIPS

★ Turn off lights when you leave a room.
★ Don't leave the water running while you brush your teeth.
★ Compost vegetable scraps instead of throwing them away.
★ Buy products with less packaging.
★ Recycle everything you can!

People save energy by using compact
fluorescent lightbulbs.

Our field team has arrived in Colorado to see another special house. We are up in the mountains. It's beautiful here! The pine trees smell good, and the meadow is full of wildflowers. This house does not have electricity coming to it through power lines. This kind of house is called "off the grid." The grid is the name for the power lines that connect homes to power plants across the country.

Off the Grid

Homes that are off the grid use solar and wind power for energy instead. These homes cost more to build, but their owners don't pay power bills. That savings will eventually pay for their solar and wind systems.

The house is similar to the house we saw in New Mexico. It was built to save energy, but it still needs power. This house gets most of its power from solar panels. Solar power can heat water and make electricity.

Hot Water and Solar Cells

Regular water heaters use electricity or natural gas to heat up water. Solar water heaters use heat from the sun. A big, shiny solar collector sits in the sun in front of the

Installing solar panels is another way to provide a house with energy.

house. Water moves through tubes in the solar collector and gets warmed up when the sun shines on it. Then that water is pumped inside to use for warm showers and to clean dishes.

Off-the-grid houses can still have electric lights and televisions. They use solar cells to change energy from the sun into electricity. Solar cells are made from silicon—the same stuff sand is made of. Solar cells can make electricity only when the sun is shining. Batteries store this energy, so we can turn on lights after the sun goes down.

People who live in solar-powered homes have to be careful about how much energy they use. Solar panels and batteries are expensive. Most people don't have more of them than they really need. Families who need more energy can also buy wind turbines.

Energy from Wind

Wind turbines have blades that spin when the wind blows, just like a toy pinwheel. Homeowners can buy small wind turbines to make their own electricity. Wind power is great because it is free once you have the turbine, and it doesn't cause pollution. However, even small wind turbines are expensive.

This Colorado mountain house has a small wind turbine out back. It stands up high on a tower. Its curved white blades spin in the wind. It makes enough electricity for the owners to run some appliances and a computer.

At our next stop, we'll see some huge, amazing wind turbines in Wyoming. ★

A wind turbine provides this house with energy.

Our last site visit was earlier today. We have learned so much about alternative energies. Today our field team visited a wind farm in southern Wyoming. The wind turbines here are huge. They are 300 feet (91 m) tall and have giant rotating blades. They can be seen from miles away.

This part of Wyoming is one of the windiest places in the nation. That wind is used to make a lot of electricity. The electricity from this wind farm is made without creating pollution.

Wind Farms and Wildlife

Lots of wind farms are built on cattle ranches. The cattle don't mind the wind turbines at all. They graze right underneath them.

Birds do have a reason to worry about wind farms. The fast-moving blades of wind turbines can kill birds, and sometimes bats and bugs, too. Newer wind turbine designs have slower-moving blades. The slower blades are safer for animals. Some new turbines are called vertical wind turbines. They are funny looking and have no blades at all. Some of them look like giant eggbeaters!

Fields of wind turbines create a lot of energy.

People in Wyoming worried that wind farms would harm wildlife. They didn't allow wind farms to be built where the sage grouse lives. There are not many sage grouse left. No one wants these beautiful birds to become extinct. Scientists and wind turbine companies must work to make wind turbines as safe as possible for animals.

Vertical wind turbines are less dangerous for birds.

WHY NOT USE HYDROELECTRIC POWER?

Hydroelectric power gets energy from river water. Water trapped behind a dam escapes through turbines, making electricity. Hydroelectric power does not create pollution. However, the dams can kill fish. Fish, including salmon, migrate upstream to lay their eggs. Dams block them from their breeding grounds. Some salmon are becoming extinct because of dams.

Energy without Pollution

We were very excited to learn how to use energy without causing pollution. By using alternative energies, we can save money and protect Earth. It's a great feeling to help ourselves and the planet at the same time. ★

MISSION ACCOMPLISHED!

Great job! You have learned new things about energy. You've discovered that we don't have to waste energy. We can do better. We can use alternative energies instead of fossil fuels. Fossil fuels will run out some day. Plus, they cause pollution and climate change. Now you know ways that we can use less of them. Congratulations on a mission well done. We're all inspired to use solar and wind power!

CONSIDER THIS

Consider other ways you can help save energy resources. By asking yourself more questions about saving energy, you might just start a mission of your own!

★ Why are people so worried about our energy supply?
★ Why is it important to use renewable sources of energy?
★ How might climate change affect people?
★ What steps can you take to save energy?

What can you do to save energy?

alternative energy (awl-TUR-nuh-tiv EN-ur-jee) a clean energy source such as solar or wind power

atmosphere (AT-muhss-fihr) the air that surrounds Earth

carbon footprint (KAR-buhn FUT-print) the amount of carbon dioxide a person produces in a year

compact fluorescent (KOM-pakt flu-RESS-uhnt) a lightbulb made to save energy and last a long time

fossil fuels (FOSS-uhl FYOO-uhlss) fuels including oil and natural gas that are the remains of ancient plants and animals

greenhouse effect (GREEN-houss uh-FEKT) warming caused by energy from the sun getting trapped behind glass or in the atmosphere

greenhouse gases (GREEN-houss GASS-uhz) gases that trap heat in the atmosphere

hydroelectric power (hye-droh-i-LEK-trik POU-ur) power that is generated by moving water

insulation (in-suh-LAY-shun) a material that traps heat

natural gas (NACH-ur-uhl GASS) a gas found deep underground; a fossil fuel used for heating and cooling

pollution (puh-LOO-shuhn) harmful substances released into the air, soil, or water

thermal mass (THUR-muhl MASS) the ability of a material to store heat

wind turbine (WIND TUR-buhn) a machine that generates power from the wind

BOOKS

Amsel, Sheri. *The Everything Kids' Environment Book: Learn How You Can Help the Environment by Getting Involved at School, at Home, or at Play.* Avon, MA: Adams Media Corp., 2007.

Petersen, Christine. *Alternative Energy.* New York, NY: Scholastic, Inc., 2004.

WEB SITES

EPA Environmental Kids Club.

http://www.epa.gov/kids/air.htm

Fun activities and experiments for kids and teachers.

Zero Footprint Youth Calculator.

http://calc.zerofootprint.net/youth/neew/results

Calculate your carbon footprint and learn how to shrink it!

FURTHER MISSIONS

SHRINK YOUR CARBON FOOTPRINT!

Get your family together and make a plan to shrink your carbon footprint. See how many ways you can all save energy. You might even challenge a friend's family to see who can save the most! You can calculate your own carbon footprint at this kid-friendly Web site:

http://calc.zerofootprint.net/youth/neew/results

FEEL HOW A SOLAR WATER HEATER WORKS

Fill a water balloon or get some water into a garden hose. To make sure some water stays in the hose, run it for a few seconds. Shut it off and quickly put the nozzle up on a high surface so the water does not spill out the end. Put the garden hose or water balloon in the sun and leave it there for a couple of hours. When you come back, feel the sun-warmed water as you sprinkle it on some plants!

INDEX

ABOUT THE AUTHOR

Courtney Farrell taught biology and microbiology for ten years at Front Range Community College in Colorado but is now a full-time science writer. She has a master's degree in zoology and is interested in conservation and sustainability issues. She lives with her husband and sons on a ranch in Colorado.

ABOUT THE CONSULTANTS

Jeff Clark is an associate professor of geology at Lawrence University, where he serves as chair of the environmental studies program. He received his doctorate from the Johns Hopkins University and he has undergraduate degrees in geology and environmental studies from Middlebury College.

Gail Saunders-Smith is a former classroom teacher and Reading Recovery teacher leader. Currently she teaches literacy courses at Youngstown State University in Ohio. Gail is the author of many books for children and three professional books for teachers.